alone
AND
Content

Inspiring, empowering essays
to help divorced and widowed
women feel whole and
complete on their own

Gwenn Voelckers

DEDICATION

To all the courageous and resilient women who embrace
their independence and accept time alone as a gift, not a
burden; an adventure, not a hardship; and an opportunity to
rediscover and honor their true, awesome selves.

CONTENTS

Build your home in your heart
and be forever sheltered.

— Anonymous

ACKNOWLEDGMENTS

Publishing this collection of essays has been a wonderfully fulfilling and heartwarming team effort. My deepest appreciation goes to the following people who helped make it possible:

First, Sally Ward, of Ward Leadership, my role model and personal coach, who helped me uncover and understand what I was meant to do with my life. Time spent working with her was life changing, and I'll be forever grateful for her empathy, skillful guidance, and encouragement.

My "workshop women" for generously sharing their personal stories, struggles, and triumphs. Their courage touched me deeply and inspired not only the essays in this collection but also my ongoing commitment to helping women live alone with confidence, peace, and joy.

Wagner Dotto, publisher and editor of *In Good Health*, the newspaper in which my monthly column appears. He invited me to become a contributing columnist over a decade ago and has been my biggest fan ever since. This book would not exist were it not for Wagner's foresight and support.

My talented editor, Robin L. Flanigan, who thoughtfully led me through a positive and collaborative editing process that resulted in a better book. Her discerning eye, advice, and keen writing instincts improved every essay on every conceivable level. Her edits were offered with diplomacy and a delicate touch, always careful to preserve my voice. Robin taught me to become a better writer along the way. She was a complete joy to work with, and I now call Robin my friend as well as my editor.

I am indebted to my volunteer "readers," who generously took time to read the book draft and provide candid feedback. Thanks also to my talented graphic designer, Rebecca Nolen, who visually brought the narrative to life.

Finally, and from the bottom of my heart, I want to thank my sister and best friend, Anne Palumbo, whose love, encouragement, and sense of humor have been a source of inspiration throughout this writing adventure. She is a much-loved columnist and book author, and her intelligent, insightful edits have strengthened each essay. My champion and kindred spirit, Anne makes me laugh, she makes me think, and most of all she inspires me to be my best self in words and in life. We should all be so lucky to have an "Annie" in our lives to cheer us on, to offer unwavering support, and to fill us up with happiness (not to mention killer guacamole).

INTRODUCTION

You've picked up this book, so chances are you're feeling a bit lost or lonely, maybe even a little scared – especially if a long-term relationship has ended.

Whether you've lost a partner through divorce, death, or other life circumstance, you may be struggling to regain your confidence and zest for living. Many discover that after years of focusing on the needs and desires of others, they've lost their "true north" and have disappeared around the edges.

As a divorced woman, I know how painful it can be to find yourself living alone. I also know it's possible to reclaim your life, to determine who you really are, and to turn living solo into an adventure of self-discovery and personal growth.

Whether only for a year or for the rest of your life, getting good at living alone will improve your chances of finding happiness. It might even improve your chances of finding a new, healthy relationship, if that's what you desire. When you feel better about yourself – more fulfilled and self-assured – the world opens up and becomes more inviting. With increased freedom and independence, you can rewrite your life story on your terms.

Thanks to some good advice from my mother after my marriage collapsed ("You've got to start living again and stop waiting for Prince Charming!"), I set out to create a wonderful life on my own. It has been an eye-opening, life-changing journey – one that has inspired me to help others regain their footing and find contentment.

Within these pages you'll find hope and inspiration, maybe even a few laughs, and lots of down-to-earth tips and advice I've offered through my monthly newspaper column and the Living Alone workshops I've led since 2005.

You'll discover new ways of thinking – and living – to rebuild your life and help you feel whole and complete on your own.

HOW CONTENT ARE YOU?
A QUIZ

Merriam-Webster defines contentment as "the state of being happy and satisfied."

This dictionary definition sounds like a nice way to feel, doesn't it? Oh, if we could just snap our fingers and be happy with who we are and what we have. Wouldn't life be grand?

I've had the privilege of meeting and talking with a lot of women and men who live alone, and our conversations often turn to the subject of contentment: how to find it, how to keep it, and how to find it again once it has been lost.

Those on their own often feel a lack of something in their lives, and many have trouble letting go of a craving for things to be different.

I know. I've been there.

For years after my divorce, I had trouble seeing the good in myself and in my life. But with time, intention, and practice, I was able to stop yearning for what I didn't have and start appreciating what existed right in front of me.

It all began with an important first step – taking a hard look at myself.

I'm no expert in survey design, but I created the simple quiz below to help you assess where you are on your own road to contentment.

1

HOW CONTENT ARE YOU? Circle the choice that best answers the questions below:

1. If asked, how many positive personal qualities of yours come immediately to mind?
   A. 5 or more
   B. 1 to 4
   C. Nothing really comes to mind.

2. How would you describe your home?
   A. Very "me" – I've made it my own!
   B. It's fine. I keep meaning to redecorate but just haven't gotten around to it.
   C. It's a place to sleep.

3. How would you describe your success in letting go of old ways of thinking and of negative thoughts or behaviors that keep you anchored in the past?
   A. I live in the present; it's full steam ahead!
   B. I still go "back there" from time to time.
   C. I can't let go; I obsess about the past.

4. Could you imagine planning a trip by yourself and traveling alone to a favorite destination?
   A. In a heartbeat!
   B. Maybe someday
   C. I can't imagine that.

5. Does the thought of going alone to a cafe for a cup of coffee or grabbing a bite to eat in a local restaurant alone feel perfectly comfortable – even enjoyable?
   A. I do it all the time.
   B. Occasionally, but I'm not at ease.
   C. I'm just not ready.

6. Do you exercise, get enough sleep, and stay on top of health screenings?
   A. Of course
   B. I know I should, but I don't always take care of myself.
   C. I'm too preoccupied to think about my health.

7. How often do you reward or pamper yourself by taking some time just for you or by purchasing that little something special you've had your eye on?
   A. As often as I can!
   B. Sometimes, but I tend to put others' needs first.
   C. I can't remember the last time I pampered myself.

8. Can you imagine your life without a special someone on your arm?
   A. I would enjoy sharing my life with someone special but could also find contentment with my "family of friends."
   B. Maybe, but not for long; I feel incomplete without a "one and only."
   C. Life doesn't feel worth living when I'm not in love.

Turn the page to calculate your score and review your results.

YOUR SCORECARD

Give yourself:
3 points for each answer in column A
2 points for each answer in column B
1 point for each answer in column C

8 points: Contentment may feel elusive at the moment – beyond your grasp. But it can be found. You may benefit from talking with a professional or your pastor. Help and encouragement might also be found in grief support groups and other gatherings that offer emotional support.

9–16 points: You experience feelings of contentment, but you know there's more to be found. Continue to stretch yourself. Reach out to others. And "try on" healthy pursuits outside your comfort zone. Success and achievement breed contentment. You might also find inspiration and a needed jump start in workshops, classes, and lectures devoted to personal growth and development.

16+ points: Good for you – what you have is precious. Being content with yourself opens up all kinds of possibilities. It enables you to feel peace and joy, whether you are alone or with others. It is an invaluable inner springboard on which you can launch all things imaginable!

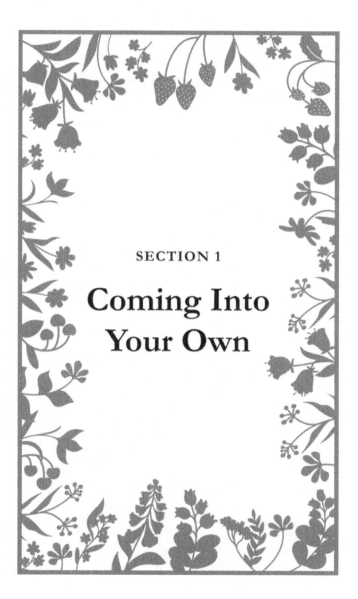

SECTION 1

Coming Into
Your Own

GROWING THROUGH LOSS

Within a span of eight years, I lost my mother, my father, my dog, a dear friend to a rare cancer, and then my brother, who left this world far too soon at age 60. I was barely recovering from one loss when I was faced with another.

I'm still trying to make sense of it all.

Just as living with a spouse doesn't guarantee "happily ever after," living alone doesn't guarantee safe shelter from life's losses and heartaches. Loss comes with living. It's inevitable and sometimes predictable. And not all loss is bad. That's what I've come to know.

Whether a loss is caused by death, the end of a relationship, or other life circumstance, most of us struggle to comprehend and cope with the emotions that result. That certainly was the case for me after my divorce.

The breakup of my marriage was the first major loss in my life, and my recovery was slow and painful. It was also transforming. Loss became my teacher, and I learned profound life lessons about grief, self-compassion, and ultimately acceptance.

If you are in the throes of loss, perhaps my reflections will help soothe some pain and ease your anxiety. While there's no best way to manage loss, I've discovered some things along the way that may help you feel a sense of renewal and hope.

Loss is as personal as it is profound. Fortunately, in my times of loss, I have had my family, friends, and therapist here to remind me that each of us is unique and each of us manages loss and grief in our own, individual ways.

I was not urged to "move on" or "find closure." I appreciated everyone who simply let me be me, on my timetable – to cry or not, to return to work or not, or to enjoy an evening out, when I was ready for company and in need of a good, hard laugh.

Loss can inspire honest expression. As a young adult, being emotive was not my style. Stoic is probably how most people (including myself) viewed me. But as my losses grew, so did my need and desire to express my true feelings. And now I wouldn't have it any other way. My losses have inspired me to be more real, more spontaneous, and more authentic. I wouldn't change that for anything.

Loss can facilitate self-awareness. This was especially true for me, in terms of getting in touch with myself and some unfinished issues and unresolved feelings. When I thought about what I wished had been different or what I would have liked more of in a relationship, my losses helped me clarify my preferences and priorities.

My brother's premature death inspired me to examine my own life. Was I living in the moment? Appreciating every day? Embracing my friends and family? His passing inspired me to be more present, to listen harder, and to reveal myself more fully to those I love.

Loss welcomes a good listener (and some forgiveness). Understandably, people often don't know what to say to a friend or loved one who has experienced a loss. When unwanted advice and careless remarks came my way, I tried my best to forgive those whose intentions were good but whose words hurt. Mostly I appreciated those who sat with me, let me cry, and listened with empathy and compassion.

Loss can sometimes use a change of scenery. I have always believed that the mind and body are connected. When the clouds roll in and sadness visits, I seek out what restores my faith and renews my energy. For me that means spending time in nature. Turning off my cell phone and going for a long walk in a beautiful, peaceful place helps me regain my perspective. I'm reminded that "spring" will return. Life can be good again.

Loss reminds us of what really matters. My late mother, who shared many of my losses, didn't hesitate for a moment when asked what was important to her. "Family," she said, unequivocally. I couldn't agree more.

Grief and loss can teach us so much. For me, clarity about what matters has been one of the most valuable lessons.

If you are struggling with loss and feelings of isolation, I encourage you to draw loved ones close. Whether it be a friend, family member, counselor, or pastor, reach out and invite help and support into your life.

Know that feeling better is within reach for all of us, especially if we seek self-awareness, keep our hearts and minds open, and have the courage to explore and express our feelings.

WHAT YOU CAN DO TODAY

Ask yourself:

What have my losses taught me about myself?

Now jot down one thing you will do today to fully experience and accept your losses in a way that feels right for you.

_____

_____

_____

_____

_____

_____

_____

_____

BANISH NEGATIVE THINKING

I'm convinced that our attitudes, thoughts, and beliefs determine the lives we live. And experience has taught me that a positive outlook can make all the difference for those of us who live alone.

If you don't like the results you are getting in your life, take a look at changing the beliefs that are producing those results. *You have choices.* Choose to focus on your strengths and gifts. Use this time on your own to define what you want and to create a life consistent with your goals and values.

To get there, to feel the way you want to feel, embrace a set of beliefs that will inspire and guide you.

Here's how:

Reframe your thoughts. While negative thoughts can be informative, an internal dialogue that is persistently pessimistic can stop you in your tracks. If that is happening for you, I encourage you to redirect your thinking.

A negative thought – such as thinking something must be wrong with you because all your friends are married and you're not – can be reframed into something more positive and productive.

Instead, you could say to yourself, "I may not feel on top of the world today, but I am resourceful and determined. Over time, I'm confident I can create a rewarding life full of people and experiences that bring me joy."

Turn them off. If those negative tapes keep rolling, give yourself a good five minutes to bask in those depressing thoughts...*then stop the tape* and redirect your thinking to something more positive. Some people even set a timer. When the alarm rings after five minutes, they know it's time to move on.

Throw them out. Crazy as it sounds, physically tossing negative, nagging thoughts into the trash (or the ocean, a lake, or a burning fire) can be liberating. Studies have shown that the act of writing down a negative thought and throwing it away can result in a more positive outlook. Next time your negative thoughts pay you a visit, write them down and give them the heave-ho.

Be your own best friend. Talk to yourself as if you were your own best friend. Acknowledge your feelings, and then offer yourself some good advice. Remind yourself how wonderful you are and how many people appreciate and count on you.

Avoid complainers, whiners, and moaners. Negative people will bring you down, reinforce your fears, and undermine your confidence. Instead, nurture relationships with people who love life regardless of their marital statuses. Enthusiasm is contagious. Put yourself around people who make you feel good about yourself and about being alive.

I have found that it's next to impossible to create healthy changes and undergo personal growth when immersed in negative thinking. Living without a spouse or significant other need not be a period of diminishing opportunity. Shift your thoughts, and this can be a time of expanding possibilities.

WHAT YOU CAN DO TODAY

Ask yourself:

What negative thoughts are getting in the way of my personal growth?

Now jot down a few positive thoughts you intend to embrace every time a nagging negative thought enters your mind.

_____

_____

_____

_____

_____

_____

_____

_____

_____

REDISCOVER YOUR TRUE SELF

There is no magic pill for getting good at living alone. Like mastering any new skill, it requires effort and lots of practice.

A good place to begin is to determine who you really are and what you really want for your life. Let go of any "shoulds" or other people's agendas.

Sounds simple, but for those coming out of a long relationship, rediscovering "who you really are" can be daunting. After years of focusing on the needs and desires of a spouse and family, many discover that, somewhere along the way, they have lost their own identities.

Rediscovering yourself and identifying those things that bring joy and meaning into your life can turn living alone into an adventure of the spirit. Once you identify and begin pursuing your own interests, you'll find that time by yourself no longer feels empty and that the silent spaces between events become more bearable – even enjoyable.

To help you get back in touch with your true self:

Look Back and Reach In

Identify those things that fully engrossed you as a child or that today completely consume you – those things that make you feel complete, as though nothing is missing. These are your "loves." These pursuits reveal your true self.

SPEND TIME WITH THESE QUESTIONS

1. What hobbies did you pursue as a child that gave you joy? What did you do or perform particularly well or (perhaps secretly) take pride in?

2. When do you completely lose yourself? What are you doing when time flies?

3. What are the kinds of activities you enjoy when you have time to yourself, such as when you are on vacation? How do you spend your time when no one's watching, when you are just being you?

4. When you open a newspaper or magazine, what articles interest you most? Could they hint at a hidden passion?

Take Action

Based on the answers above, identify one step (even a small step) you can take *now* to reconnect with a past pursuit or delve more deeply into an existing interest.

When I went through this exercise years ago, I rediscovered a part of me that I had neglected – without realizing it – for years. That part was my creative side. While thinking back over my life, I remembered how much I had enjoyed art classes as a kid, and I recalled the hours I had spent engaged in pencil drawing and other artistic endeavors.

Then, when I looked at my life as an adult, I realized how very few creative outlets I had incorporated into my daily and weekly routines. So I set out to make a deliberate change and to reincorporate creative expression into my world.

The result? I now enjoy craft projects, love redecorating my home, and in the summer months, design and tend gardens that burst with color, texture, and fragrance.

Get to know yourself all over again. When you identify the things you love to do and then do them, it's easier to feel more integrated and in touch with who you are – and who you want to become.

When that happens, living alone becomes secondary to *living fully*!

WHAT YOU CAN DO TODAY

Ask yourself:

What do I love to do? What pursuit makes me feel complete, as if nothing is missing?

Now jot down one thing you will do today to pursue this love.

_____

_____

_____

_____

_____

_____

_____

_____

_____

TENDING THE GARDEN WITHIN

It wasn't until I purchased my country home, with its overflowing flowerbeds, that I unwittingly discovered my love of gardening.

I was in a do-or-die situation: either I do the work or they die – all those gorgeous peonies, columbine, daisies, pink poppies, and more. Not on my thumb!

So I got busy.

I picked up my trowel and dug right in. I became a self-taught, homegrown gardener and have never looked back. Now I'm completely hooked. Come springtime I get restless with anticipation and can't wait to get my hands and knees dirty.

Gardening is all about caretaking and tending and love. Slack off, even for a few days, and all things unwelcome show up and take root.

By osmosis, gardening has taught me how to take better care of myself. Fertile ground exists in each of us, and a little tending can produce beautiful results. Here's what I have learned:

Plan. The garden of your dreams begins in your imagination, followed by careful planning. Diagramming a garden helps you avoid planting bulbs on top of bulbs or mistaking a poppy for a weed. Likewise, envisioning your life goals and committing them to writing will help you flourish and grow.

Cultivate. Good soil that has been properly prepared for planting promotes healthy, deep roots and rewards you with abundance. The same thing happens when you add essential ingredients to the foundation of your dream life – ingredients that will nourish all that follows.

Plant. So many choices! Revisit your plan and embed your carefully selected seeds with a tender, loving touch, being careful not to overcrowd or plant more than you can manage.

And remember: we reap what we sow. Plant a rose, and you get a rose; plant a dandelion, and you get a dandelion. Seed your future with healthy choices that promote well-being.

Water. Plants need water to grow and thrive. Tears are like water for our souls. Crying can be cathartic, healing, and helpful.

Feed. Plants bloom and more fully bear their bounty with the addition of fertilizer and nutrients. We can reap the same rewards when we nourish our inner selves.

Weed. We all need room to breathe and positive space in which to blossom. Weed out the negativity and any dream-stealing toxins that contaminate your life, dash your hopes, or spoil your fun. When you pull out the bad, you can more easily focus on the good.

Prune. When weeding is not enough, a major pruning may be just what the arborist ordered. A job, relationship, or home that no longer satisfies or meets your needs may need a hard look. It may be time to pick up that pair of "life loppers."

Mulch. Mulching keeps weeds at bay, keeps the ground moist, and returns nutrients to the soil. Mulch offers a blanket of protection in the same way that regular doctor appointments, insurance, and safety measures protect our lives.

Wait. When you exercise patience and enjoy the gradual unfolding of a flower, an idea, or a friendship, your life can be savored and more deeply appreciated. Each year I look to my garden to remind me that growth takes time.

Enjoy. Before you know it, your labor of love and patience will pay off. Take pleasure in the transformation as the colors, textures, and fragrances emerge. Too often we fail to "stop and smell the roses" in our gardens and in our lives. Admire what you've accomplished. It's reason to celebrate!

Why not grab a spade and join me? Beauty, growth, and an energizing sense of renewal are waiting for us season after season.

WHAT YOU CAN DO TODAY

Ask yourself:

Am I tending my inner garden?

Now jot down one thing you will do today to take care of and nurture yourself.

_____

_____

_____

_____

_____

_____

_____

_____

_____

OVERCOMING LONELINESS

I was listening to my favorite oldies-but-goodies radio station when a familiar tune transported me back to junior high school. The year was 1967, and I was distraught about being soundly dumped by my seventh-grade heartthrob.

The song, "One," had just been released by Three Dog Night, and I spent days wallowing in its sad refrain: "One is the loneliest number that you'll ever do." I was certain I would feel the heartache of unbearable loneliness for all eternity.

The song's doleful lyrics reinforce one of our greatest fears, as well as one of the oldest stereotypes of all time – that being alone, without that "special someone," means a life sentence of loneliness and despair.

But here's a question for you: Were you ever lonely in your marriage or relationship? Many people answer with a resounding "Yes."

Loneliness can and does descend on each of us from time to time, especially when we feel separated from others. What's important to remember is that loneliness is not a state reserved for single people. That single women are lonely or lonelier than their married counterparts is a myth. In fact loneliness has very little to do with being alone and everything to do with your state of mind.

The next time you begin to feel disconnected from the world, take a moment to remind yourself that your happiness is in your hands and that there are positive steps you can take to overcome loneliness and feel better.

Consider these:

Get moving. Get up, and out of the house. A brisk walk or quick car trip can put you in a different frame of mind and lift your spirits.

Pick up the phone. Ask a friend or neighbor for advice, or put yourself in touch with someone to simply say, "I'm thinking of you." A quick call, text, or e-mail can set good things in motion and change your mood.

Do something for someone else. Drop someone a note of congratulations. Bake some goodies for your colleagues at work. Leave fresh flowers on a neighbor's doorstep. When you do things for others, you feel less alone and more a part of the world.

Rekindle long-lost friendships. Set aside an evening or some time during a weekend to reach out to an old friend or two. Send a short note by e-mail or snail mail. Briefly describe what's going on in your life, and express how much you'd like to reconnect and catch up. You'll most likely be rewarded with a response for your efforts.

Put something on your calendar. Make arrangements to dine out or see a movie with a friend, family member, or colleague. Take on the role of "social secretary," and you'll gradually feel your social circle becoming more active and interesting.

Become a joiner. Consider taking a continuing-education class or belonging to a gym, church group, dance class, or book club. Try something new, or choose a pursuit that deepens an existing interest.

I recently joined a community band for older adults. My instrument was piano (in my youth), but community bands don't typically include keyboard players. They needed a percussionist. I said, "I'm game!" It's been so much fun to learn a new instrument and to join this wonderful community of people who share my love of music.

Let go of the idea that being married is the antidote for loneliness. Holding on to this idea may make you vulnerable to relationships that are inappropriate or unhealthy. It's better to get good at managing your loneliness by choosing to engage in healthy, productive activities that expand your world, challenge your intellect, and bring you joy.

Take advantage of this unique time in your life!

WHAT YOU CAN DO TODAY

Ask yourself:

Am I feeling lonely? Do I need to remind myself that my happiness is in my hands?

Now jot down one thing you will do today to make a connection with a friend, family member, or activity you enjoy.

_____

_____

_____

_____

_____

_____

_____

_____

GRATITUDE:
EXPRESS IT IN WRITING

When my heart is gripped by loss, when I'm threatened by change, or when I'm overcome by disappointment, it's helpful to revisit – and add to – my gratitude journal. I keep my journal close at hand and use it to lift my mood and renew my hope.

Writing down and reflecting on those things for which I'm grateful is a fulfilling, healing exercise.

By focusing on gratitude, we become more aware of the positive aspects in our lives, which in turn can help shift our thinking and attitudes. A gratitude journal is one of the easiest ways to make this focus a part of your life. Here's how to get started:

Step one. Purchase a blank notebook or journal. Any kind will do, but I suggest choosing one that reflects your own individual style. Mine is a beautiful, little spiral-bound journal covered in handmade paper, with a decorative satin ribbon. It's pretty just to look at and very inviting. I keep it within easy reach on my bedside stand.

Step two. Find a time to write in your gratitude journal every day. It doesn't matter if it's the last thing you do before you go to sleep or the first thing you do in the morning. What's important is that you find a quiet time when you can be alone with your thoughts and feelings. I've found I do a better job of keeping my journal when I make a commitment to write at a regular time each and every day.

Step three. Make your list personal, and try to come up with at least two blessings. Nothing may come to mind immediately, but if you take your time and keep thinking, you may be surprised at what surfaces.

For instance, if you decide to write in your journal at night, think back over your day. Identify those things, people, or places that made an impression on you, great or small. It could be the sound of a breeze through the trees, a new assignment at work, or a stranger's warm hello in passing.

Step four. Start every day with an open heart and with an intention to see the positive and the possibilities in life. If you bump into an obstacle, try to appreciate the opportunity it presents to overcome it. When you focus on wonderful things, wonderful things begin to happen. It reminds me of the law of attraction. Your positive thoughts and energy can become a magnet and draw even more positive thoughts and energy in your direction.

Document these meaningful moments in your journal.

Step five. Make your writing come to life by adding photos, quotes, scripture, or magazine clippings. I love embellishing my journal with favorite sayings and simple sketches.

So, what might you find in my gratitude journal? Here's a peek, in hopes that what I have to share might inspire you to capture your own blessings in writing:

- Being greeted every morning by my puppy's adorable face and wagging tail

- A friend calling to ask, "Free to do something tonight?"

- Reading about compassionate, tolerant people who embrace diversity

- A good haircut and highlights

- Growing my own garlic

- The thrill of a thunderstorm

- Learning to play the snare drum and weekly band rehearsals

- My dear girlfriends whose friendships keep me sane

- A bonfire, any time of year

- My morning walks and the kind drivers who wave "hello"

- Music and movies that tug at my heart

Going deeper, I'm grateful for:

- My parents' influence, which I feel in the deepest part of me, even in their absence. I'll forever be grateful for my mother's strength, sensitivity, and caring touch; her big smile and warm hug when I came to visit were always so reassuring and welcome. I am also thankful for my father's creative, entrepreneurial ways whenever I pick up a tool, dare to take a risk, or find the courage to be direct in my dealings with others.

- My sister Anne's gigantic heart, sense of humor, and passion for her family and friends. She knows me like no other and still enjoys my company! When I'm with her, I'm inspired to be a better person (and a sillier one, too). Our relationship is precious and brings me so much joy.

- My dear friend Terry's generous and determined spirit. When confronted with life's uncertainties, he perseveres with resourcefulness and conviction. We share a wonderful friendship, and I smile when I think of his patience, warmth, and engaging personality.

Even after years of keeping a gratitude journal, I am struck by how the straightforward act of writing down what I value and love every day can change my world for the better. It's simple. It's free. And it has been transformative.

WHAT YOU CAN DO TODAY

Ask yourself:

Do I tend to focus on what is lacking in my life?

Now jot down one thing you are thankful for today, then describe a simple pleasure or relationship that fills you with happiness.

_____

_____

_____

_____

_____

_____

_____

_____

_____

SECTION 2

Overcoming
Challenges

FEELING NEGLECTED AND FORGOTTEN?

Have you been feeling neglected and forgotten? Have you been sitting alone, feeling sorry for yourself, and wondering...Where is everybody? Why isn't anybody calling? What's going on?

Since losing my mother, I've had bouts of the blues and have spent too much time alone. Sometimes the loss overwhelms me, and I lose my oomph for doing much of anything.

This loneliness reminds me of the painful months after my divorce, when I isolated myself in my apartment and avoided friends and family. Eventually my phone stopped ringing, and the weekends stretched out before me like a long, lonely highway.

I know slumps happen. Life ebbs and flows. So when I started feeling neglected and began blaming others for my sorry social calendar, I knew an attitude adjustment was in order. Specifically I needed to remind myself that my life is in my hands – that *I'm* responsible for how lonely (or not) I am, and that I'm in charge of how large or small my life is.

So what did I do? I picked up the phone, called a girlfriend, and made plans for the weekend. Then I picked up the phone again and left a text message for my sister, asking her to give me a call.

And I didn't stop there.

I worked up the nerve, rehearsed a few words, and made a third call to a neighbor who also lives alone. I asked if he wanted to take a walk later that evening. He asked for a rain check, but that was OK. We made plans to take a walk the following week, which gave me something nice to anticipate.

Next I shifted over to my computer and sent out a few "Hi, how are you?" e-mails to friends, inviting them over to see (and admire!) my newly renovated powder room I'd been madly painting and redecorating – and wanted to show off. Why not, right? It's rewarding to hear "oohs" and "aahs," and sometimes we need to create opportunities for positive feedback.

I was on a roll, and it became downright fun to see how easily I could change my circumstances by doing just a few small things – by converting my newly adjusted attitude into action.

Within days, my phone started ringing again, my inbox began to fill up, and I had entered a few social events into my calendar. Life felt better!

Part of what motivates me when I find myself in a slump is a passage I found in a sweet little book called *Living Alone and Lovin' It*, by Barbara Feldon. In one particularly helpful chapter on loneliness, she recounts a heart-to-heart she had with an "older and very wise friend" named Leo. She was brooding about being lonely and shared how much she wanted to feel loved and protected again, the way she felt when she was a child.

Leo responded quite bluntly: "But you're not a child and don't have a child's needs. A child is in danger without company because it's helpless, but an adult has access to any need imaginable: food, medicine, companionship. All an adult has to do is pick up the phone…"

Good friends can be such a help! Especially when they tell it like it is. Barbara was energized by Leo's no-excuses straight talk, and indirectly so was I. As adults, we can exercise choices; we can choose to stay in a slump or choose to pick up the phone. Start dialing, and you'll be surprised how fast your feelings of self-pity and abandonment can evaporate.

Little by little your world will expand, with one connection spawning another, and another, and yet another.

WHAT YOU CAN DO TODAY

Ask yourself:

Am I feeling sorry for myself?

Now jot down one thing you will do today to connect with others.

_____

_____

_____

_____

_____

_____

_____

_____

SET GOALS, BUILD
CONFIDENCE

My self-esteem took a real nosedive after my divorce. I felt exposed and embarrassed, as if my private failure at a relationship was somehow very public. I just wanted to hide. And hide I did – in my work, in my house, in my self-help books, and from my friends.

Self-confidence can get destroyed after a divorce, even a fairly amicable one. Regaining my confidence was a slow process and painful at times but ultimately very rewarding.

The process started with baby steps.

While I am a huge believer in positive thinking, I knew intuitively that I wouldn't be able to *think* myself into feeling better about myself. I realized it would take work to rebuild my confidence one step and one success at a time. That's when I discovered the incredible power of goal setting.

During the dark days following my divorce, I found that writing tasks down and checking them off helped me get through the day. At the time, because even simple things seemed insurmountable, my to-do list was pitifully basic: get dressed, make my bed, water the plants, etc. I would add just *one* item at a time, do it, then check it off (versus making a long list to start, which would have completely overwhelmed me).

Remarkably (thankfully!) this process began to have a real and positive impact on my day and self-esteem. Committing things to writing seemed to have miraculous power. My to-do list motivated me, held me accountable, and enabled me to track my progress and successes.

It didn't take long before one good day was followed by another, and it continued from there. My sense of accomplishment was as energizing as it was fulfilling. I began to feel stronger and more self-assured.

I still create a to-do list every day, and now I enter several items at a time. I get a confidence boost when I accomplish one of my minigoals and check it off the list. This practice has been so rewarding and self-affirming that I now use the same process for bigger life plans and projects.

In fact I created a "Goal Worksheet" for myself that captures what every good goal should be: written down, specific, time bound, and achievable.

Here's an example:

Goal statement:

I will plan and go on a solo retreat – a restorative weekend alone to recharge my batteries, rediscover my center, and enjoy some quiet time to think, reflect, and dream.

Action steps and timetable:

DAY 1
I will share my travel goal with a few friends and ask for suggested retreat destinations within an easy driving distance.

DAYS 2–5
I will review my options, make a decision, and reserve a place to stay for a weekend in late October.

DAY 6
I will inform family members (and a close neighbor) of my plans, including my travel destination and how to reach me.

DAY 7
I will make arrangements for pet care.

DAYS 8–9
I will spend a few days researching restaurants, checking out things to do, and finding a spa for a much-anticipated massage!

DAY 10
I will pack light, including emergency supplies, a journal, and a good book, which may come in handy as a pleasant diversion while dining alone.

DAY 11
I will prepare healthy snacks for the road, carefully review driving directions, check tire pressure and oil, and then fill the gas tank.

DAY 12

I will take off early, excited and proud to be leaving on my mini-adventure.

Goals can give your life direction and purpose – and they can put passion into your everyday existence.

It may take some time before you regain your footing and feel a boost in your self-esteem. Chances are you'll encounter some bumps and take some detours along the way. But I have found that setting and accomplishing mini-goals, and eventually larger life goals, is key to regaining self-confidence.

WHAT YOU CAN DO TODAY

Ask yourself:

Do I have a goal I would like to accomplish? Am I willing to do what it takes to regain my self-esteem?

Now jot down *one thing* you will do today to achieve that goal and build your confidence.

_____

_____

_____

_____

_____

_____

_____

_____

HEALING THROUGH FORGIVENESS

Let me start by sharing a story: After thirty-eight years of marriage, two children, and countless memories, my friend arrived home from work one day to find a handwritten note on her nightstand. Her husband had left her to "find himself."

Blindsided, she dropped onto the bed, stunned in disbelief. She later found his clothes closet empty and his home office cleared out. With no word on his whereabouts, she racked her brain, desperate to make sense of his bizarre behavior. Had she missed something? Was he ill? And where in the world was he?

Days later her anguish was replaced by anger when she inspected his computer history and discovered that he had met someone online. He and his newfound "soul mate" had scheduled a rendezvous in Florida.

It has been years since my friend's husband left, but to hear her talk about it today is to bring everything immediately to the fore – the deep emotional wound, the humiliation, and the loss of life as she knew it. The retelling of her ordeal quickly ignites a seething anger just beneath the surface. How could he have done this to her and the kids? How could he have betrayed them?

While my friend's lingering bitterness is understandable, it is also unfortunate. By dwelling on this hurtful event and hanging on to her anger, she is allowing her resentment and hostility to fester. Left unchecked, she risks bringing negativity into current relationships and experiences or worse, letting her anger hurt the connections with the people who matter most in her life. I feel for her.

Does an abiding bitterness occupy your thoughts? Nearly all of us have been hurt by the words or actions of others somewhere along the way. The wounds may be deep, but if you don't practice forgiveness, you might end up being the one who pays the biggest price.

While it can feel almost impossible to let go of a long-standing grudge and feelings of resentment, I can tell you from experience that forgiveness can bring a measure of peace and may even make room for compassion and understanding.

I've also learned that forgiveness doesn't just happen on its own or overnight. You must *choose* to forgive. It's a process of change that requires commitment, courage, and self-reflection:

Acknowledge and share your pain. Let it all out. Share your suffering with someone you trust, and don't hold back. When there's someone there to really listen, your pain can become tolerable and perhaps more likely to dissipate.

Empathize with the person who hurt you. This may not be easy, but remember that none of us is perfect. The person who hurt you may have been acting out of self-preservation, an unspoken fear, or pain of his or her own.

Take a hard look at yourself. We all know there are two sides to every story. What was your role in the breakdown of your relationship or in whatever has contributed to your resentment? Taking personal responsibility for our own words and behavior, and, importantly, their results, is an essential part of forgiveness – not just of others, but of ourselves.

Holding on to a victim mentality may serve to validate an unhappy situation, but it can also keep you mired in anger and thoughts of revenge.

Embrace the benefits of forgiveness. Forgiveness can be empowering. It can set you free from the past and release the control the offending person has had in your life. There are health benefits as well when you carry a lighter emotional load.

Focus on the future. Rather than focusing on the past and your wounded feelings, seek out positive, healthy relationships and experiences. Put your energy into finding beauty and kindness around you. A future filled with gratitude and appreciation can help diminish painful memories.

When you are ready, actively choose to forgive the person who hurt you. Remember, you can forgive the person without excusing the act. Forgiveness is not about condoning. It's a gift you give yourself – to be released from bitterness and vengeful thinking.

Reinforce your forgiveness with a symbolic act. In my workshops, participants take part in a "letting go" ceremony in which they symbolically release anger, negative attitudes, and unhealthy behaviors into my wood-burning fireplace. Many capture their thoughts in writing and find some relief in seeing their past hurts go up in flames. Symbolic acts such as this can help the healing process.

As you let go of anger, grudges, resentments, and thoughts of revenge, you may no longer define yourself and your life by past hurts and grievances. When you embrace forgiveness, you are embracing the promise of renewed compassion, kindness, and gratitude. Even some tenderness.

Forgiveness can be healing and set you free.

WHAT YOU CAN DO TODAY

Ask yourself:

Is a past resentment or grudge keeping me from moving on with my life and being the person I want to be?

Now jot down one thing you will do today to forgive yourself or someone else.

_____

_____

_____

_____

_____

_____

_____

_____

_____

DOLLARS AND SENSE:
SUPPORTING YOURSELF

"I'll end up alone and penniless."

That sums up one of the biggest fears divorced and widowed women have when they find themselves living alone – by choice or by chance – in midlife.

I discovered this fear around money management when I interviewed more than fifty women when preparing the curriculum for my first Living Alone workshop. Managing their finances was a real challenge for many of them.

The problem is this: once a woman is out of the financial loop, she often remains there, which puts her at a real disadvantage. Her knowledge of and self-confidence around money matters becomes very diminished.

Simply put, when one partner controls the finances, the other can be left in a vulnerable position when a relationship ends. This vulnerability was expressed over and over again in the interviews I conducted, which is why I devote a portion of each workshop to getting one's financial house in order.

My financial advisor helped me identify a few essential steps for gaining financial control:

Come out from under the covers. Ignorance is not bliss when it comes to financial management. You need to find the courage to get up close and personal with your financial circumstances. I avoided looking into my financial mirror for years until the fear of *not* doing anything was greater than the fear of facing reality.

In my case, fear turned out to be a blessing in disguise – a real motivator. It prompted me to get my act together and seek help. There's no time like the present to take charge of your money and your destiny.

Find your stuff. David Bach, renowned financial expert and author of *Smart Women Finish Rich*, says it best: "Getting organized is one of the keys to financial security. It begins with finding your stuff." Before you can plan your financial future, you need to figure out where you stand financially in the present, and that starts with gathering together all your financial documents in one place.

I cleared out a file drawer in my desk, purchased new hanging file folders, and labeled the files according to the instructions in David Bach's book. It didn't take as long as I thought it would, and I felt a great sense of accomplishment once I had everything collected within easy reach. And guess what. This simple step helped me feel more in control. Almost immediately my fears began to lessen.

Get help if you need it. Once I had my "stuff" together, I was in a much better position to make sense of my financial situation. I continued to work through Bach's book, but found I needed a real person to help me take the next steps and make more progress. That's when I engaged the help of a financial representative, who helped me align my spending, saving, and investing with my needs and priorities. He has been an invaluable coach and motivator.

If you're more self-directed on educating yourself about money matters, there are excellent resources available in books and magazines, and online.

Peace of mind and a sense of empowerment are the rewards for those who get their finances in order. Solid information, personal discipline, and good help from a trusted advisor can turn financial uncertainty into financial security. With increased confidence and awareness, you can better protect your future and more fully embrace the pleasures of living alone...with a little left over to splurge on something special just for you!

WHAT YOU CAN DO TODAY

Ask yourself:

Are my fears about money keeping me from taking charge of my future?

Now jot down one thing you will do today to get your financial house in order.

_____

_____

_____

_____

_____

_____

_____

_____

_____

ASKING FOR HELP

It's not the load that breaks you down,
it's the way you carry it.

— Lena Horne

A ride to the doctor's office. Extra hands to move heavy furniture. An emergency dog sitting request.

Giving and receiving help from my friends and family has proved to be a wonderful way to strengthen bonds. I have learned time and again that asking for help brings blessings, not burdens.

Many people – and often those of us who need it most – find it hard to reach out and ask for assistance in times of need. The reasons are numerous, but my experience tells me that lots of women who live alone avoid asking for help because they fear being seen as weak or vulnerable.

I know that after my divorce I was reluctant to ask for help. I wanted to show the world that I was perfectly fine, thank you very much. I avoided asking anybody for anything, determined to muscle through on my own. It led to isolation and pointless hardships.

And the biggest shame? Not asking for support kept me distant from friends and family. I denied myself (and them) the chance to connect on a genuine and meaningful level. Looking back it is clear to me that my healing and personal growth came more slowly as a result.

I encourage you to let go of any excuses *not* to ask for help, in favor of being true to yourself and to those who love and want to support you.

How can you help yourself?

Be honest. Take a moment to reflect on what keeps you from asking for assistance. Could it be pride? Do you think you'll be seen as incapable or inadequate? Are you concerned about being a bother? Or would asking for help force you to acknowledge that, indeed, you need it?

Redefine what it means to be strong. Everyone needs outside aid from time to time, and seeking help on your terms is not a weakness. In fact the strongest people are often those who have the courage to admit they need reinforcements. I've always admired this quality in others. Real strength is knowing your personal limitations and having the confidence to recruit assistance when necessary.

Have some faith. Believe that people truly *want* to help. Just think about how you'd respond if a friend, family member, or coworker asked for a helping hand. You likely wouldn't hesitate; you might even feel slighted if not asked, especially if someone you cared about was having real difficulty. Know that others, too, want to be there for friends and family in need.

Take a chance. When you choose to open yourself up and expose your authentic self, you are taking a risk. That's a good thing! When you are "real" like this, you have an amazing opportunity to cultivate deeper, more meaningful connections with others.

Make the request. First put some thought into where you could really use some support; then ask for help with one specific item. It could be something as simple as weeding a garden bed to something as important as identifying a financial advisor. If you think you'll feel awkward making the request, you might start out by saying, "You know, I'm not very comfortable asking for favors, but I wonder if you might be able to help me with something."

Express your gratitude. You know this, of course. A heartfelt thank you in person or in writing will be warmly received by the person whose help you have accepted. No need to go overboard. Remember, most people want to help others and don't expect to be compensated for doing a good deed.

Offer help in return. Because giving can be as gratifying as receiving, make it known that you are available to return the favor. Better yet, find opportunities to offer help. We all have gifts and can be of great assistance to one another.

Take it from me...life *can* be better, just for the asking.

WHAT YOU CAN DO TODAY

Ask yourself:

Am I afraid or too proud to ask for assistance?

Now jot down one thing you will do today to get help for something you need.

_____

_____

_____

_____

_____

_____

_____

_____

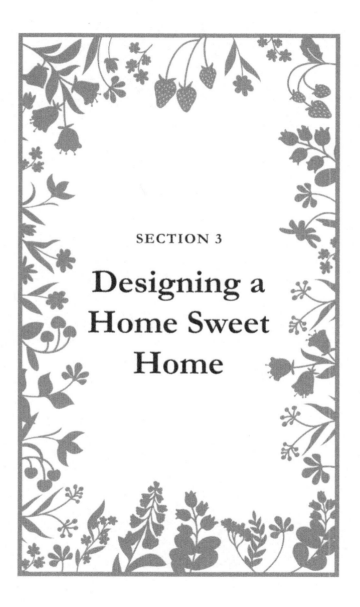

SECTION 3

Designing a Home Sweet Home

YOUR HOME: MAKE IT
YOUR OWN

When Dorothy in the *Wizard of Oz* closes her eyes, clicks her heels, and whispers, "There's no place like home," she is hoping to be transported back to that place of security, warmth, and love…and into the arms of her adoring Auntie Em. Ahhh, the comforts of home.

Creating a soothing home for myself after my divorce was an essential part of starting my life over as a woman on her own. Intuitively I knew I needed to walk through my new front door and into my very own "warm embrace," a place where I would be surrounded and inspired by all things familiar and friendly.

So I set out to create a retreat – a personal sanctuary where I could feel safe and sound. It was what I needed at the time, but since then my home has evolved into much more than a nurturing place. My living space has become a pallet of personal expression, where I have gained a true appreciation for the value of having, as Virginia Woolf so eloquently stated, a "room of her own."

With yourself as your sole guide, turn your kitchen, living room, and bedroom into portraits of your true nature – what you value and what you love. Making a home your own becomes an adventure in autonomy and a chance to explore and express – perhaps for the first time in your life – your own tastes unleashed, without compromise.

The process can be liberating. Energizing. Even healing.

One of the first things I did when I bought my home (after I tore out the green shag carpet) was frame and display photographs of family and friends. I wanted to see their faces when I entered a room, to be reminded of good times and the love that surrounds me. That was only the beginning of a series of decisions that made being in my own space not just pleasant but also more enchanting and satisfying than I could have imagined.

Paying attention to your surroundings can have an immediate and lasting impact on how you feel about yourself and about living alone.

To get started:

Follow your heart. With no one around to second-guess decisions or veto preferences, you are free to express yourself in the colors, fabrics, art, and accessories you choose. If you don't know where to start, think about what colors draw you in. What hues do you prefer in your garden? What colors make up your wardrobe?

Eliminate the negative. Anything that makes you feel bad when you look at it should be trashed or repaired. Ratty dishtowels, old lampshades, and faded curtains, for example, can dampen your mood and erode your self-esteem. Don't underestimate the negative power of unsightly or outdated objects.

Emphasize the positive. Surround yourself with images and objects that lift your spirit and reinforce both who you are and who you want to become. In addition to photos and fresh flowers, I adorn my living space with original pieces of art and artifacts I collect on my travels. I believe in the symbolic nature of objects and find inspiration in what surrounds me.

Reduce the clutter. Corners, closets, and drawers crammed with useless stuff all contribute to negative energy, according to the tenets of feng shui, the ancient Chinese practice of organizing space to achieve harmony and balance. I'm a true devotee of this concept and have seen it make a positive difference in my life. For a good book on the subject, check out Karen Kingston's *Clear Your Clutter with Feng Shui.*

Decorate with your senses. Is the hollow sound of loneliness bouncing off your walls? Is there a musty smell wafting up from the basement? Are your cabinets sticky? When I started paying attention to more than just visual aesthetics, my home became even friendlier territory. Transform your solitary space by creating an atmosphere filled with your favorite music, pleasing aromas, and clean surfaces.

Your home can become an oasis of independence and autonomy – a place that's unconditionally yours, absent of compromise. Claim it. Once you make your personal space your own…there's no place like home!

WHAT YOU CAN DO TODAY

Ask yourself:

Am I paying enough attention to my environment and the impact it has on my sense of self and well-being?

Now jot down one thing you will do today to create your own "warm hug" when you walk through the front door of your home.

_____

_____

_____

_____

_____

_____

_____

_____

_____

CREATE A SAFE HAVEN

It was a Saturday night, around 10:45 p.m. when I returned home from a night out with friends. Life was good – until I walked through the front door. I could tell something was amiss the moment I stepped inside. Things were slightly out of place. The lid on one of my little decorative boxes was askew. A door was ajar. My dog was jumpy.

Feeling uneasy I poked my head into the living room and saw nothing unusual there. Whew! Then I made my way upstairs, and what I found took my breath away. My bedroom and spare room were completely torn apart: clothes and personal effects strewn everywhere, drawers yanked open and emptied into the middle of each room, closets were ransacked. Even the lampshades were crooked. It looked like a scene out of a scary movie.

Trembling, I called 911. A dispatcher told me to get out of the house immediately, cautioning that the burglar might still be present. I hadn't thought of that! I grabbed my cell phone, left the house, and waited in my locked car for the police to arrive. While waiting I called a friend and asked him to come over.

Needless to say, that experience was a terrifying wake-up call for me. Realizing I needed to pay closer attention to my safety and security, I talked with police, insurance consultants, and other reliable safety advisors, and I put into practice multiple precautions to protect myself and my property.

I pass them on to you here:

If you're going out for the evening, do the following:

- Make it look and sound as if you're still home. Leave the TV on and use automatic timers on lights and radios.

- Turn on interior and exterior lights. Light is the enemy of those with misguided intentions.

- Lock all doors and windows. You'd be amazed how many people don't do this!

- Keep your purse, wallet, money, jewelry, and other valuables out of sight. (At the least out of view from a window.)

If you're going away for an extended period of time, do the following:

- Again, make it look and sound as if you're still home with the help of automatic timers on lights and radios.

- Give a spare key to a neighbor you trust, rather than hiding one outside your home. Let this same trusted neighbor know of your travel plans, itinerary, and how to reach you.

- Stop mail and newspaper delivery. Better yet, have a neighbor or friend sign on for pick-up duty. Having someone you trust making daily visits to your home when you're not there also offers added protection.

- Make arrangements to have your grass mowed or snow shoveled, depending on the time of year.

- To be extra cautious, ask your local police to keep an eye on your home.

Make long-term investments in home security:

• In addition to your front and back porch lights, consider installing motion-detector lights outside your home.

• Consult a good locksmith to have high-quality deadbolts and other locking systems installed on your doors and windows.

• Eliminate hiding places outside your home. Cut back bushes and shrubs, especially those that block windows.

• Consider installing a security system, especially one with a loud alarm and flashing lights that will attract immediate attention. The door or lawn sign from your alarm company may help deter a break-in all by itself.

While there are never any guarantees, of course, using common sense and some simple precautions can reduce your risks of a break-in that could result in theft, property damage, or worse. Let's face it, crime is a reality, and women living alone need to take extra measures to protect themselves.

Be safe, not sorry!

WHAT YOU CAN DO TODAY

Ask yourself:

Have I taken the appropriate safety measures to protect myself and my property?

Now jot down one thing you will do today to reduce your risk of a break-in.

_____

_____

_____

_____

_____

_____

_____

_____

_____

PREPARE A PLEASING
"TABLE FOR ONE"

When you invite a friend over for dinner, do you hand her a bowl of cereal and ask her to stand at the sink? Do you give him a spoon and a jar of peanut butter? Not a chance, right? You probably whip up something nice and simple, create a pleasing place setting, and sit down to dinner at the kitchen or dining room table.

While living alone gives you the freedom to dine as you please (one of its many pleasures), I don't recommend a steady diet of Cheerios. Treat yourself instead as you would treat a good friend you've invited for dinner.

Why? Because you're worth it. Because you will feel better about yourself, both physically and emotionally. And because you will be sending a message to others – other single friends, adult children, even a parent – that self-care and treating yourself with respect is important.

Besides, eating well has all kinds of benefits. And what better way to start enjoying those benefits than by creating an inviting "table for one" in your own home?

Stock your kitchen with healthy food. It's so much easier to put a healthy meal on the table when good food is plentiful and junk food is in short supply. I'm fully aware of my own downfalls (ice cream, cookies, and chips), and do not regularly stock these items in my kitchen. Instead I have on hand a good supply of fruits and vegetables, prepackaged salad greens, frozen entrees, and easy-to-grill fresh cuts of meat and fish.

Indulge your senses. Stimulate your appetite by preparing an item or meal with a wonderful, delicious aroma. I boost many a solo dining experience with a little butter and chopped onions in my iron skillet. The aroma invites me into the cooking process, and within minutes the worries and stresses of my day start to melt away. I also try to incorporate foods with a variety of textures and color – soft, chewy, crisp, and firm – into each meal.

Select the best seat in the house. While eating in front of the TV may be the perfect choice on some occasions, I encourage you to find dining spaces inside or outside your home that offer more inspiration. Chances are you'll appreciate the change of scenery. Consider that special nook where the sun filters in or the table by the window with the great view. Mix it up, experiment with different settings, and see how much better it feels.

Set the stage. Have some fun with your table setting: Put down a placemat, use a cloth napkin, bring out the wine glass, turn on some enjoyable music, and position a good book or magazine within reach. I often light a candle. If you've never set the stage like this, it can feel contrived the first few times, but stay with it. Over time I believe you'll find it enjoyable and relaxing.

Enjoy your own company. When you eat alone, you are with someone who approves of your cooking techniques, appreciates the candle you lit, and knows that life and food are to be enjoyed. Cherish this quality time with yourself.

Creating a pleasant "table for one" can help make you feel more energetic, happier, and healthier. It's a great opportunity to focus on yourself and to nourish your body and spirit at the same time. Bon appetit!

WHAT YOU CAN DO TODAY

Ask yourself:

Has mealtime become an unrewarding, sometimes unwelcome, experience for me?

Now jot down one thing you will do today to start a new dining routine – one that will nourish both body and spirit.

_____

_____

_____

_____

_____

_____

_____

_____

_____

KEEP IT SIMPLE

I just love the sight of laundry on a clothesline, fluttering in the breeze on a sunny summer day. It reminds me of times gone by: my happy childhood in Ohio, my mom folding laundry, my dad tending his garden, and all things old-fashioned and wholesome.

On a recent road trip through the countryside, I was so taken by the colorful clothes and linen hanging outside to dry that I returned home with a mission: to install my own backyard clothesline.

For less than $30 dollars, I purchased the essentials: rope, pulley, hooks, and cleat. For a few dollars more, I equipped myself with wooden clothespins and a canvas drawstring bag. The installation of my clothesline between two mature oaks took less than an hour.

I couldn't wait to do a load of laundry! I eagerly anticipated the simple bliss of hanging my pillowcases, towels, and T-shirts on the line and watching them sway in the gentle wind.

Beyond the nostalgia, I could also appreciate that air-drying my clothing was good for the earth. In a small way, I would be reducing my household carbon footprint, and that idea sat well with me and my conscience.

The experience reminded me of the value of simple living and how easy it is to get back to the basics – something that's even easier for those of us who live alone and can make all our own decisions.

I'm committed to leading a simpler life, a more natural existence. How about you? Below are a few things we all can do:

Accumulate less stuff. If I don't absolutely need it or love it, I don't buy it. That's my new MO. I live in a small home, and I've discovered that things need to be stored, sorted, dusted, and otherwise dealt with. Some of it needs to be insured. Other stuff needs to be repaired. Almost all of it requires some investment of time and money, both of which I want to use more wisely. This brings me to my next tip:

Let go of more stuff. Goodwill, VOA, Savers, and the Vietnam Veterans of America are my new best friends. I'm clearing out the clutter and sharing my gently used clothing and household goods with people in need and others who enjoy a bargain.

I've come to learn that these organizations are so much more than their storefronts. They use their profits for so much good: for housing, for humanitarian causes, for disaster relief, and to help people all over the globe become more self-sufficient. Every donation made has the potential to make a positive difference in someone's life.

Repair, reuse, and make do. My old toothbrushes have become cleaning tools, shoeboxes are now storage containers for photos, and old picture frames have become "shabby chic" mirrors. These are just a few examples. I love making something new and beautiful out of something old or discarded.

I've been guilty of wasteful ways, and I'm now very focused on using up what's "on the shelf" or "in the tube." I'm also very determined to make do with what I already own. I feel proud when I act responsibly and make good decisions that lead to fewer purchases.

Enjoy the real thing. I grow my own tomatoes, onions, garlic, peppers, beans, and herbs. My dad was my gardening guru. Following in the footsteps of his own father, my dad taught me how to plant, when to plant, what to plant, and how to take care of a garden.

Beyond the cost-saving benefits of gardening, I feel healthier and more alive when I'm tending plants. There is something incredibly therapeutic about kneeling next to my raised garden beds and cultivating the soil at day's end when the sun is setting. Away from my computer, I enjoy the peace and quiet and find deep satisfaction working with my hands.

Be clear about what matters. My "keep it simple" goal has inspired me to look inward and really think about what I value and what I want my life to be about. I want to simplify things, because by doing so, I'll open up time and resources for spending quality time with my family, my friends, and myself.

When life is simpler, I can keep these priorities front and center. Instead of shopping or troubleshooting or worrying about my things, I can embrace what matters and live a life that reflects what I care about most: being with those I love.

Keeping it simple can bring us more joy, more harmony, and more peace of mind. And that can lead to deeper contentment and happiness. It's as simple as that.

WHAT YOU CAN DO TODAY

Ask yourself:

Am I making life more complicated than it needs to be?

Now jot down one thing you will do today to simplify your life.

_____

_____

_____

_____

_____

_____

_____

_____

_____

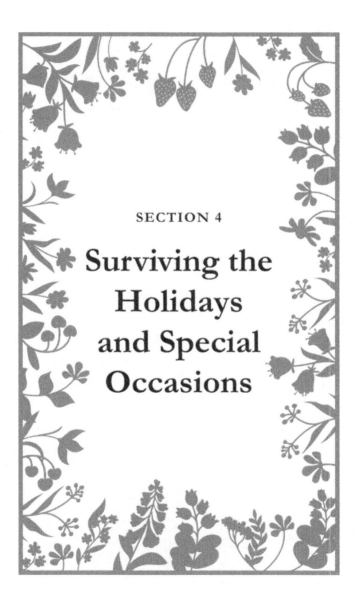

SECTION 4

Surviving the Holidays and Special Occasions

A DOZEN "DON'TS"
FOR THE NEW YEAR

I've shared lots of "do's" in the past to help people live alone with more success. Here are a few "don'ts" – some lighthearted – that may also help you on your journey toward contentment in the coming year:

Don't isolate. Get up, get dressed, lose the PJs or sweatpants, and get out of the house (or get on the phone). We humans are social animals; we're meant to be with others. Solitary confinement is for criminals, not for people who live alone. Stay connected!

Don't go on a shopping spree to fill an emotional void. Your savings account will thank you.

Don't make cereal your main course for dinner. Well...maybe on occasion. But as a general rule? Nope. Create a nice place setting, fill your plate with something healthy, light a candle, pour yourself a glass of wine or cranberry juice, and enjoy some well-deserved time to yourself. A favorite magazine or book can make for a nice dining companion. Bon appetit!

Don't label yourself a loser just because you are spending Saturday night alone. It's not the end of the world. It doesn't define you. Stream a Netflix movie, or clear some clutter, and call it a night. If the prospect of a Friday or Saturday night alone is too difficult, reach out to a friend today and make plans for next weekend.

Don't put too much stock in that dreamcatcher. If you find yourself wide awake in the middle of night fighting demons, you might try meditation, journaling, or aromatherapy. I fill my diffuser with lavender oil and do some deep breathing while I repeat the phrase, "Sleep is healing."

If that doesn't do the trick, I get up and prepare myself some warm milk or herbal tea. I return to bed with fingers crossed and eyes closed. If all else fails, talk to your doctor.

Don't avoid dancing lessons because you don't have a partner. Good teachers know how to incorporate singles into their classes by making introductions or by partnering with single members to demonstrate steps. Lucky you!

Don't jump into someone's arms out of loneliness. Feelings of desperation can make you easy prey for someone with dubious intentions. It's a risky place to be. Getting good at living alone will build your self-esteem and improve your chances of meeting someone who appreciates your strengths, not your weaknesses.

Don't get behind the wheel after a night out with friends, drowning your sorrows. No explanation needed.

Don't be afraid to travel alone. Some of my best trips have been taken with my favorite traveling companion: myself. I create my own itinerary, go at my own pace, and meet all kinds of interesting people along the way.

Even a small jaunt can boost your confidence. On your own you'll discover your resourcefulness, ability to solve problems, and capacity to spend some time alone. It can be an enlightening adventure in self-discovery.

Don't decline an invitation because it means walking in alone. You can do it. Seek out the host upon your arrival. This strategy gives you a game plan, as soon as you walk through the door. If the host is occupied with other guests, you can always get in line at the refreshment station. You'll be engaged in conversation before you know it. Be yourself, be sincere, and be curious about others. Go and have fun!

Don't act your age. You are free and unencumbered. What better time to spread your wings, be silly, and otherwise express your glorious, outrageous self? Put yourself with people who make you laugh. (For me that's my sister.) Keep your sense of humor – after all, life can be funny.

Don't take these "don'ts" too seriously. You are in the best position to decide what to do or not to do – no shoulds, musts, or other people's agendas. That's one of the best benefits of living alone.

Don't I know it!

WHAT YOU CAN DO TODAY

Ask yourself:

Don't I deserve a better life?

Now jot down one thing you will do today to get this year off to a great start.

_____

_____

_____

_____

_____

_____

_____

_____

_____

VALENTINE'S DAY CAN BE SWEET FOR SINGLES, TOO

Oh, it was just so disheartening.

I couldn't walk into a store, open a magazine, or even shop online in February without being bombarded with images of candy hearts, flowers, and pink teddy bears.

Starting in January the countdown to Valentine's Day begins in full force, and it's no wonder that those without a "special someone" dread what many (including Hallmark) consider to be the most romantic day of the year.

What's a single person to do?

Before drowning your sorrows in a box of Godiva chocolates, consider these tips for surviving the day dedicated to amour:

Adopt a new attitude. Take the broadest possible view of Valentine's Day, and decide it's not just a day for couples, but a day to celebrate love in all its glorious manifestations: love of self, love of family, love of friends, and – one of my favorites – love of pets! I already have my eye on a little heart-festooned collar for Scout, my lovable Springer Spaniel.

Make a decision to embrace Valentine's Day with grace, confidence and humor.

Express your love. Send cards to people you care about, buy one of those cuddly pink teddy bears for your favorite niece, connect with someone with whom you've lost touch, or treat your officemates to some bagels (with cherry cream cheese) and coffee. Even better, surprise your colleagues down the hall.

Have fun and laugh. Why not? It's just a day. Invite some of your single friends over for beer and pizza, or agree to meet anywhere that's not sporting a Valentine's Day theme. Raise a glass, and toast to your independence, your freedom, and your triumphant escape from the commercialism of this "holiday." Valentine's Day is only depressing if you let it be. Have some fun with it.

Do something for someone else. One of the best ways to avoid a downward "woe is me" spiral is to think about others in need and how you might brighten their day. Consider baking a little goodie for a neighbor who lives alone, calling your uncle who lost his wife last year, or committing one of those random acts of kindness.

Spend Valentine's Day celebrating your relationships with those you care about, work alongside, or spend time with. Chances are you'll make someone's day.

Do something for yourself. If you didn't get around to making any New Year's resolutions, consider making February 14 your new New Year's Day. Resolve to quit smoking, renew your membership at the gym (better yet, go to the gym), schedule your annual physical, organize your paperwork, or vow to do something that will improve your outlook, your health, and your future.

This year on Valentine's Day, I went online to join Nextdoor, a free online network that connects neighbors with one another. I now have an easy way to find a dog sitter, learn about an upcoming block party, hear about any safety issues in the area, and get referrals for home-maintenance projects.

And my final tip? Now, don't laugh. On February 13 (or before), purchase a small candy or decorative heart. Place the heart on your bedside stand the night before Valentine's Day. That symbolic heart will be waiting for you on the fourteenth when you wake up, reminding you that you are loved by the person who matters most – yourself!

WHAT YOU CAN DO TODAY

Ask yourself:

Am I am dreading Valentine's Day?

Now jot down one thing you will do today, in anticipation of Valentine's Day, to express your love and kindness toward yourself and others.

_____

_____

_____

_____

_____

_____

_____

_____

_____

LEARN TO SAY "NO, THANK YOU"

In addition to counting your many blessings on Thanksgiving (and throughout the year), I encourage all those who live alone – as well as those who don't – to say, "No, thank you," to things that get in the way of your personal growth and happiness.

Say, "No, thank you," to feeling sorry for yourself, which only perpetuates the cycle and makes you feel sad and needy. Chances are you've survived a lot this year and have gained new self-knowledge and growth. Feel good about that.

Say, "No, thank you," to self-imposed isolation. We humans aren't meant to be alone. We're social creatures and need one another for companionship, stimulation, and inspiration. Pick up the phone!

Say, "No, thank you," to an unmade bed, kitchen clutter, and any other depressing signs of discontent at home that make you feel lousy about yourself, conjure up bad or sad memories, or zap your energy. Clean up and create a pleasing, harmonious home.

Say, "No, thank you," to languishing on the couch. The more you move your body, the healthier it gets, and the better you can feel, physically and emotionally. The good news? Studies show that it doesn't take an enormous amount of physical exercise to achieve health-enhancing results. About thirty minutes a day of walking, swimming, jogging, or biking can have positive health effects.

Say, "No, thank you," to overspending and credit-card debt. Think twice before you make a purchase. Do you really need it? And can you really afford it? Since most everyone spends more on credit cards, you just might want to *leave home without it*. Increased financial security, peace of mind, and a sense of empowerment are the rewards for those who spend within their means.

Say, "No, thank you," to entering into a relationship to avoid feeling lonely. It puts you at risk. When you're lonely and desperate, it shows. It makes you vulnerable to the advances of someone with less than honorable intentions. Get good at being on your own. A content and confident you is more likely to attract a quality companion.

Say, "No, thank you," to skipping meals or eating takeout over the kitchen sink.

Say, "No, thank you," to negative thinking. Negative self-talk (e.g., "I'll never meet anyone" or "I hate my weight") unwittingly becomes a self-fulfilling prophecy. Become aware of negativity, stop it in its tracks, and replace it with a positive thought.

Say, "No, thank you," to friends who complain all the time and bring you down. Instead of helping themselves or the world, complainers spread gloom and doom. Who needs it? Hang out with people who make you smile, lift you up, support you in your efforts to overcome challenges, and generally make you feel good to be alive.

Say, "No, thank you," to letting yourself go. How you look says a lot about you – and how you value yourself. Spend a few minutes on your appearance, put on a pleasant expression, and watch the world open up. When you care about yourself and your appearance, you radiate vitality. It's intriguing. And it will draw people and compliments to you.

Say, "No, thank you," to feelings of helplessness. Children are helpless; most adults are not. Learning to master things around the house – from minor repairs to hiring a roofing contractor, from planting a garden to making lasagna from scratch – can be a real source of satisfaction and pride. It can also make you an even more interesting, confident, and well-rounded person.

Say, "No, thank you," to that second helping this Thanksgiving. As tempting as another piece of pumpkin pie might be, you'll feel better the day after if you pass it up. You will feel proud of your self-discipline, enjoy more energy, and have more room for leftovers later on.

Happy "No-Thanks"giving!

WHAT YOU CAN DO TODAY

Ask yourself:

Am I sabotaging my own growth and potential?

Now jot down one thing you would like to say, "No, thank you," to and express how that would make you happier.

_____

_____

_____

_____

_____

_____

_____

_____

SPENDING THE HOLIDAYS ALONE

The prospect of spending the holidays alone can send a cold chill through even the most independent among us. And it's no wonder. All the hype for traditions that tout *togetherness* can leave divorced, widowed, and single people feeling alone and disconnected.

The "holiday blues" can take hold with a vengeance.

You can beat those blues with a change in attitude by deciding to make this holiday season a good one. Take advantage of this special time of year to spend some quality time with yourself, create memorable moments with friends and family, and help those less fortunate.

To get in the spirit:

Slow down. Better yet, stop what you're doing altogether. Ask yourself what the holidays really mean to you. Rebirth? Hope? Family time? Gratitude and goodwill? Revisit your most deeply held beliefs about the season and make a conscious decision to participate in the holiday rituals that align with your values and spiritual underpinnings.

Be realistic and give yourself a break. For those who live alone, some degree of loneliness can be considered normal during the holidays. It's a good time to remember that feelings of loneliness aren't terminal, nor are they reserved for single people.

Loneliness has very little to do with *being alone* and everything to do with your state of mind. Remind yourself that your happiness is in your hands and that there are positive, healthy steps you can take to foster it.

Create new holiday traditions. This is especially important if you are bemoaning the loss of the irretrievable traditions of a former life. Consider instituting your own signature traditions – a new cookie recipe, for example, or a gathering of single friends at your place.

Volunteer and express gratitude. When you give of yourself, you reap two big rewards: developing connections with people who share your spirit of giving and helping those in need. Volunteering, especially at this time of year, can nurture your soul and make a meaningful difference.

If volunteering doesn't fit into your schedule right now, there are plenty of other ways to express your gratitude and ability to make others feel special. Consider baking holiday goodies for your colleagues at work. Or leave a little something on a neighbor's doorstep.

When you are doing for others and counting your blessings, you can transcend yourself and your current circumstances. The result? You might feel less lonely – more a part of the world and of this season of giving.

Be the instigator. Identify a holiday concert or event you'd like to attend, and invite family or friends to join you. For example,

I purchased two tickets to the Christmas From Vienna concert, performed by the Vienna Boys Choir at a local concert hall, before I'd decided whom to invite. That was part of the fun! The concert was on my calendar, and I could look forward to surprising a friend with an invitation.

Seeding your future with anticipated events will give you something to look forward to during this time of year.

Decorate your home. Do it for *you*. It will help put you in the spirit of the season. Hang a wreath on your door. Accent your mantel. Bring the holiday inside your home and feel its essence inside your heart.

Invite people over. No need to do anything elaborate. Even having just a few friends over for brunch or to watch a holiday special on TV can fill your day with warmth and cheer.

Send out holiday cards. Take this occasion to say hello and make connections. I love getting an unexpected card from a long-lost friend and delight in tracking down and sending out season's greetings to those who might be surprised to hear from me.

Include yourself on your gift list. This is a good time of year to spoil yourself with a little comfort. Snuggle up with a new bestseller. Schedule a massage or pedicure. Treat yourself to something you've had your eye on.

Let go. This is key. Let go of the notion that you need to be married or in a romantic relationship to enjoy the holidays. Life is all about personal connections, and there are plenty to be found in friends, family, neighbors, colleagues – even people you meet in passing.

Feeling a little lost this time of year is only natural. I struggled for years until I made an effort to get into the spirit. Never forget that you have choices: you can choose to be with people rather than isolate, or you can choose to appreciate what you have rather than focus on what you're missing.

I promise you this: embrace even half of the tips above, and you'll experience a merrier, more meaningful, and less lonely holiday.

WHAT YOU CAN DO TODAY

Ask yourself:

Am I going to let my "woe is me" attitude ruin another holiday season?

Now jot down one thing you will do today to make your holidays more about others by bringing joy and cheer into their lives.

_____

_____

_____

_____

_____

_____

_____

_____

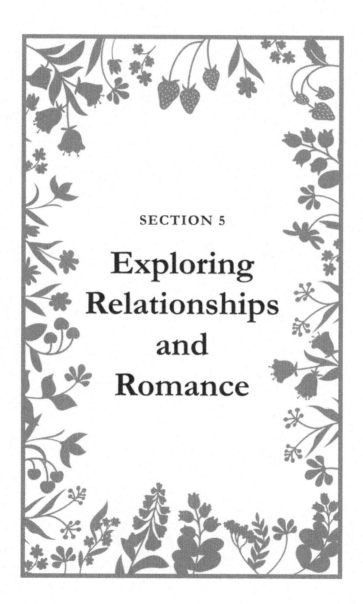

SECTION 5

Exploring Relationships and Romance

SOCIALIZING IN A
COUPLES' WORLD

The fear of walking into an event by yourself or the discomfort of being a "fifth wheel" can keep lots of single women home on the weekend.

Though this was years ago, I still remember the dismal details that followed an invitation to a distant relative's wedding. It wasn't long after my divorce, and I was – amazingly, under the circumstances – excited about going. I like weddings and was looking forward to reconnecting with some friends and relatives I hadn't seen in some time. Plus it was a reason to dress up and get out of the house.

I pulled up to the church, parked, and sat in my car. After assessing the parking lot, looking for familiar vehicles, and faces, I waited...and watched. I watched one happy couple after another walking in, holding hands, laughing, and looking so in love. I could feel my blood pressure rising and my courage faltering.

I started to think, "What am I doing here?" And then the litany of "poor me" statements began to take over. I sat there in my pretty dress and pumps, unable to muster the courage to enter the church alone. I started up the car and returned home to my empty apartment.

Disappointed with myself, I vowed not to let something like that happen again. I wasn't going to miss out on life's experiences just because I was single. In that moment I resolved not to let my fears and insecurities keep me confined to my home and a safe circle of women friends.

Learning to do things solo and to actually enjoy myself took time, practice and, frankly, some guts. Fortunately, I figured out few things along the way that made it easier. Here are some of the most important:

Overcome self-conscious thinking. Part of what kept me from going out to eat or to a movie by myself was my concern about what people would think of me – or more honestly what *I thought* they would think of me. Did I have no friends? Was I undesirable company? Or on the prowl? Overcoming self-conscious thinking was essential to moving forward and out of my house.

What do *you* think when you see a woman walking into an event alone or sitting by herself at Starbucks reading the paper? Do you assign negative attributes to her? Probably not. You likely don't give it a second thought. Or maybe you secretly admire her confidence and ability to enjoy her own company. Keep this in mind the next time your fears and doubts keep you from venturing out alone.

Expand your social circle. If you've fallen out of the social circuit, it's your responsibility to find a way back in. You need to make the first move, and one of the best ways to get back onto invitation lists is to embrace the theory of reciprocity: you invite people into your world, and they in turn, will invite you into theirs. No need to go overboard; inviting a few friends over for coffee or a cookout will get the ball rolling. Your social network will begin to grow, and before you know it, you'll find yourself enjoying the company of good friends, both old and new.

Be prepared to bump into your ex. If concerns about running into an ex-spouse or significant other at a social event keep you from accepting invitations, be prepared. Before you go, anticipate and visualize running into your ex. See yourself handling the encounter with grace and, most importantly, brevity. A few pleasantries and a polite "take care" will help you move past the encounter in a relatively quick and painless manner. Bumping into an ex may be inevitable depending on your situation, so gear up, grin and bear it, and get going on your way.

Walk in alone with confidence. Even after all these years of living alone and attending social engagements on my own, I still don't relish the thought of walking into an event by myself. In fact, to make it more palatable, I developed a five-step formula to ease my way in – and it has never failed me:

1. Pull up to the event and gather my thoughts in the car.

2. Repeat this mantra: "All I need is within me now."

3. Take a few deep breaths.

4. Remind myself to be myself and to be curious about others.

5. Enter the event and make a beeline for the host to say hello, and introduce myself to others standing nearby.

After that I can more easily enter into universally accepted small-talk subjects: books, travel, food, movies, and sports.

Feeling good about living alone often means confronting social, as well as emotional, challenges. Getting comfortable in a couples' world is among them. But once mastered, it gets easier and easier. Even fun! You will find that you again can feel warmly integrated into the world.

WHAT YOU CAN DO TODAY

Ask yourself:

Have I fallen off the social circuit?

Now jot down one thing you will do today to demonstrate that you can venture out into the world on your own.

_____

_____

_____

_____

_____

_____

_____

_____

FINDING LOVE
IN UNEXPECTED PLACES

Have you ever heard that song "Lookin' for Love" by Johnny Lee? Here's the chorus:

I was lookin' for love in all the wrong places
Lookin' for love in too many faces

Love comes in all sizes and shapes, colors and contrasts. Some love appears shiny and bright like Fourth of July fireworks. Other love comes in plain brown paper.

Few would disagree that love, in all its manifestations, makes life rich and full and worth living. But when love is defined too narrowly, it can spell heartbreak and disappointment for the woman who doesn't have a special someone in her life.

In one of my most cherished books, *Life Lessons* by Dr. Elisabeth Kübler-Ross and David Kessler, the authors make an important point: We don't always recognize love, because we categorize it, declaring romantic love to be the only "real" kind of love.

Those of us who live alone can fall prey to that way of thinking. Thanks to time, introspection, and the teachings of others, I have learned to broaden my definition of love in order to enjoy meaningful connections everywhere I go. It has made an amazing difference in my life.

Lately some of my most intimate moments have been with an old high-school friend. Both divorced, we enjoy a comfortable brother-sister relationship that is as practical as it is profound. We attend events together, hang out, help each other with household chores on weekends, celebrate birthdays, and are there for each other when life's challenges arise. While not romantic in the classic sense of the term, there is no shortage of love in my relationship with him.

I characterize this relationship as a "passionate friendship" – one in which we feel completely comfortable and able to express ourselves openly and honestly without the complications that can sometimes come with sexual intimacy.

I believe that love can be found in many unexpected places, even in incidental, accidental relationships. And I've discovered that nearly every encounter with someone, however brief, can deliver happiness and take me to a loving place.

For example, I lead a body-conditioning class once a week at my local YMCA. Some of the members have been attending my class for years. While these class members could be considered passing strangers, they have, instead, become people I care about and who care about me. "I show up because of you," one long-time member said recently. That warmed my heart.

I also have started a pen-pal relationship with an older gentleman (a regular reader of my newspaper column) who describes himself as a divorced, "rapidly aging male," a description that makes me smile. While we're not potential dating partners, I can already tell we share a love of the written word and have lots in common.

In his most recent e-mail, he shared, "I like my house and find the single life acceptable and sometimes definitely superior (though occasionally not) to anything else." My thoughts exactly!

If you are not in an intimate relationship, it doesn't mean your life can't be filled with richness, love, and special moments. Try to recognize the potential for love and intimacy in the world around you. Be yourself, and make real connections with the people you meet and interact with during your daily routines. Look them in the eye, hear what they have to say, share what's in your heart, and smile.

Count your blessings for the many opportunities that exist for human warmth, and for the magic in the connections we experience every day, no matter how seemingly insignificant. Love is the wonder that surrounds us. With an open heart, you won't miss this life-giving gift.

WHAT YOU CAN DO TODAY

Ask yourself:

Have I shortchanged myself by thinking that the only relationships that count are romantic ones?

Now jot down one thing you will do today to acknowledge and appreciate existing relationships in your life – with friends, family, and acquaintances.

_____

_____

_____

_____

_____

_____

_____

_____

_____

EMBRACING TOUCH:
AN ESSENTIAL INGREDIENT

As I write this, I can hear my new puppy, Scout, trotting toward me. She nuzzles my leg and looks up at me with her big, brown eyes, begging for attention and a little touch. My heart swells and I scratch the back of her neck. She bows her head, asking for more, and I happily oblige.

I'm such a pushover!

Scout asks for what she needs without reservation, without any shame or self-consciousness. She knows what we all know in the deepest parts of ourselves: We need touch to survive.

I'm no expert on these matters, but others are, and research has shown that touch is absolutely essential for healthy emotional and physical development. In fact, studies have shown that premature infants who are tenderly touched on a daily basis gain weight more rapidly than those who are not touched. It's because touch releases certain chemicals in the brain that, in turn, promote the baby's development.

But I don't need a study to convince me of the value of touch and affection. I have my own proof, and it's revealed to me whenever I am touched or touch another. A friend's warm hug can lift my spirits. A reassuring hand on my shoulder can hold the demons at bay. Even a handshake can be affirming.

Those who live alone can often unintentionally, almost unconsciously, neglect this vital component of a happy, healthy life. It's easy to do, especially if you have a tendency toward isolation or are without a significant other in your life. If that's the case, I encourage you to take notice.

Is touch absent in your life? Has it been weeks or months since you have felt the warmth of an embrace? When was the last time you felt the comfort of a soothing caress?

Below are a few tips to "keep in touch." They have worked for me, and it's my hope that you, too, will benefit from incorporating positive, loving touch into your life.

Become a hugger. If you're not a hugger, I might suggest you become one, even if it's outside your comfort zone. A little practice is all it takes.

Hugging wasn't natural for me. It felt awkward for me to hug relatives, much less friends. I was forever bumping cheeks in an embrace, leaning right when I should have been leaning left. But years ago I made a deliberate decision to become a hugger.

I intuitively knew I was missing out on this natural form of human expression. The good news? I got better at it over time, and life is sweeter as a result. It gave me an opportunity to convey love and friendship and accept it in return.

Volunteer to touch. The benefits of "loving touch" are not just for the ones receiving it. Those who deliver it also reap great personal rewards and satisfaction. If you look around, there are plenty of opportunities to administer positive, healthy touch to people in need.

Many hospitals have volunteer "rockers" for newborns, and nursing homes are often looking for volunteers to make personal connections with residents who may not have family nearby. Just an hour talking to a nursing-home resident, while applying hand cream, could change his or her day.

To volunteer in this way can be a healing act of kindness, one that says we are in this life together. What soothes one soothes us all.

Own a pet. A number of well-known studies have shown that petting a dog or gently stroking a cat has a calming effect on people, reducing blood pressure and heart rate and helping them feel connected and comforted.

Petting my dog Scout, or snuggling with her on the couch, has an almost-immediate relaxing effect on me. After a long day, almost nothing is as grounding as a few minutes with my affectionate pooch.

Become in touch with yourself. "Self-touch," with the goal to soothe, heal, or relieve tension is natural and can be a healthy expression of self-care and an act of self-affirmation. When self-gratification and pleasure are experienced, something profound and restorative can be the result.

Splurge for a massage. I read recently that "massage is to the human body what a tune-up is for a car." Among its many benefits, therapeutic massage can bring relief from anxiety, reduce stress, fight fatigue, and increase your capacity for tranquil thinking and creativity. If you are touch deprived, this form of safe, non-intimate touch can refocus the body's natural ability to heal and regenerate itself.

Hugging, caressing, and soothing touch are natural expressions of friendship and affection, compassion, and comfort. We all can benefit – both physically and emotionally – from good, loving touch on a regular basis. It enhances bonding and gives us a sense of belonging and well-being – important essentials for everyone, but especially for those who live alone.

WHAT YOU CAN DO TODAY

Ask yourself:

When was the last time I gave or received a warm hug?

Now jot down one thing you will do today to incorporate more touch into your life.

_____

_____

_____

_____

_____

_____

_____

_____

_____

DATING TIPS FOR FINDING
SOMEONE SPECIAL

I'm often asked whether I ever date.

My answer is unequivocally "Yes!" More often than not, people are surprised by that answer.

I like the question, because it gives me a chance to remind everyone that being successful at living independently doesn't mean abandoning the idea of building and sharing a life with someone special.

Living alone doesn't mean *being* alone. Many people satisfy their needs and desires to be with people by developing a great group of friends, including family members. Others want more and long for the exclusive domain of a romantic relationship.

If the idea of dating in midlife after the loss of a long-term relationship or marriage seems unnerving, know that that's common. I've talked with many older women who have resigned themselves to "terminal singlehood" after having tried unsuccessfully to enter the dating scene. It only takes a few disappointments and rejections to send people running for cover. But like any challenge, if you approach dating with thoughtfulness and care, a satisfying and lasting relationship is possible at any age.

I've assembled a few tips from my own experience and the experiences of others that may help you jump-start your search for a loving companion:

Define what dating means to you. If you haven't dated in years (perhaps in decades), the term "dating" may suggest the first step in a predictable path to marriage. These days, dating is, well, dating, and you can define it any way you like. Maybe you want a date for a work event. Perhaps you'd be happy with a number of companions with whom you could enjoy movies, dinner, intimacy, etc. Or you may be on a serious quest to find a new life partner. Your definition – your dating goal – will shape the style and pace of your search.

Know what you're looking for. I once read a magazine article written by a woman who detailed her experience of writing down one hundred things she wanted in a man, and then – lo and behold – having the man of her dreams stroll right into her life. Was it coincidence? Magic? Who knows? But the exercise has merit. Thinking about what you want, as well as what's unacceptable to you, will help refine your search and improve your chances of finding a compatible partner.

Be yourself. One of the advantages of being a little older is increased self-awareness and the confidence to be who you truly are. Accept and embrace yourself "as is." Pretending to be otherwise will only compromise your chances of meeting someone who loves you just the way you are.

Spread the word. If you want to meet someone, let friends and family know you're looking. Don't be apologetic about expressing your desire to find a companion. You might say: "I'm feeling ready to meet someone. Would you keep me in mind if you run into someone who might be a good fit for me?" Another way to initiate your search includes joining a matchmaking website. (If you pursue this route, be sure to take precautions to stay safe.)

Surround yourself with like-minded people. We all enjoy being with people who share our interests, and one way to kick-start your dating adventure is to attend social, educational, or charitable functions that attract the kind of partner you are looking for. Now's also the time to join clubs and groups whose members include potential partners: a book club, a hiking group just for singles, dance lessons that don't require partners, or support groups or organizations that cater to divorced or widowed women and men. To increase your chances of success, you need to get out of the house.

Have fun and keep your expectations in check. We have all suffered the occasional bad date or rejection. Try not to let that stop you from meeting new people. Dating, just like networking for a new job, can put you in the company of interesting, stimulating people. Even if your heart doesn't go pitter-patter, you'll be out in the world, expanding your experiences and circle of friends.

So give it a whirl. When you're ready, muster the courage to start the search for that special someone. You can do this!

WHAT YOU CAN DO TODAY

Ask yourself:

Would I like to build and share a life with someone special?

Now jot down one thing you will do today to meet new people in hopes of finding a potential partner.

_____

_____

_____

_____

_____

_____

_____

_____

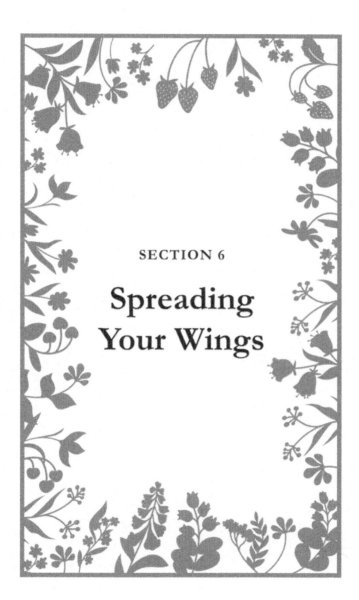

SECTION 6

Spreading
Your Wings

TRAVELING SOLO:
AN ADVENTURE
IN SELF-DISCOVERY

"Oh, I could never do that!" exclaimed a participant in my workshop. She was reacting to my enthusiastic account of traveling by myself to Paris to celebrate my 50th birthday.

She was right of course. She *would* never experience the fun and fulfillment of traveling solo – as long as she held on to that attitude.

Traveling alone, just like living alone, requires the right frame of mind to be successful and enjoyable.

Why travel alone in the first place? Why not grab a friend or two and make it a shared experience? Because the potential for self-discovery and *savoir faire* that comes with solo travel is absolutely priceless. I'm not suggesting an exclusive diet of solo travel, but I am encouraging you to consider this mode of travel for this important reason: You'll gain both confidence and wisdom from your experiences.

Here's how to get on board and make your solo adventure as rewarding as possible:

Adopt a new attitude. It starts here. You can do this, even if a spouse or significant other took care of all the travel plans and details in the past. Much like in other parts of life, you can accomplish almost anything *if you believe you can.* If you need help making sense of traveling solo, a travel agent can help.

Plan, plan, plan. I started planning my excursion to Paris three years prior to takeoff. I opened a designated "Paris" savings account and deposited $150 a month for two years. I can't tell you how wonderful it felt to return from my trip free and clear of credit-card debt. Instead I arrived back home with cherished memories and mementos of Paris, including an exquisite pair of red leather shoes and a colorful Parisian scarf that I wear all the time.

Select hotel accommodations carefully. I scoured travel literature and asked my Francophile friends about where to stay in Paris. My criteria: the hotel had to be in a good neighborhood, centrally located, very "French," and convenient to transportation. I found Hotel de Fleurie, situated on a charming side street in the heart of the Latin Quarter.

Whatever your criteria and final selection, make contact by phone or e-mail with the hotel front-desk staff before your arrival. Let them know you are traveling alone and under what circumstances. My experience taught me that hotel staff – with an understanding of your situation and knowledge of your daily itinerary – will be extra helpful and look out for you. Sharing that information can pay off in unexpected ways as well: I was surprised (and delighted!) to find a bottle of Champagne and a "Happy 50th Birthday" card in my room when I arrived.

Follow your heart. Many of us have secret hopes and dreams of visiting exotic places that have personal significance. As I approached my midlife milestone, I knew I wanted to do something really special to mark the occasion. I wanted it to be meaningful. I wanted it to be memorable. I wanted Paris! And I wasn't going to let the fact that I was divorced and on my own keep me from visiting one of the most romantic places on the planet. Don't limit your travel aspirations just because you are on your own.

Get or update your passport. This is a life staple in my book. You just never know when the opportunity for a trip of a lifetime might present itself, and you'll want to be able to grab it by the suitcase handles and take flight. (Note that it can take up to six weeks to get a passport.)

I often describe that solo trip to Paris as "the best ten days of my life." And I mean it. I spent day after glorious day exploring the City of Lights on foot, with relentless curiosity and wonder as my guide. Every quaint, historic neighborhood was more fascinating than the last, and each day more surprising and thrilling than the one before. I came home changed, fulfilled, and richer for the experience.

Whether your adventure is one day, one weekend, or one week, I encourage you to embrace the *joie de vivre* that traveling solo can inspire.

WHAT YOU CAN DO TODAY

Ask yourself:

Do I have the courage to travel without a companion – just me, myself, and I?

Now jot down one thing you will do today to start planning a solo journey, even if it's just a day trip or weekend retreat.

_____

_____

_____

_____

_____

_____

_____

_____

_____

CULTIVATING CURIOSITY

An Unforgiving Minute by Craig Mullaney is a poignant, introspective memoir of the author's evolution from civilian to US Army captain stationed in Afghanistan. Throughout the book, he details his training and military experience, infusing it with deeply personal and revealing accounts of his emotional journey along the way.

As I read his memoir, I couldn't help but think of my father, who served as a pilot in World War II. I think about all the questions I wish I had asked him when he was alive – questions that would have brought us closer and increased my understanding and appreciation of the man he was. I wish I had been more curious.

A valuable life lesson emerged as I sat contemplating the book and my father and what could have been. I began to think about the value of curiosity and how it can enrich our lives, especially for those of us who live alone. I realized that being curious can deepen relationships, expand our knowledge, serve as a great motivator, and lead to a more fulfilling life.

And so I decided to cultivate my curiosity by doing the following:

Asking more questions. Curious people dig deeper this way. They know, for example, that spending just a few extra minutes asking a colleague or neighbor about a recent vacation can be enlightening. It can reveal the unexpected. When I returned from my last trip to Paris, I was mostly greeted by the requisite "How was your vacation?" After sharing just a few details, I would hear, "Oh, that's nice," signaling a tidy end to the conversation.

One of my curious colleagues, however, was full of questions. I was touched by her genuine interest and enjoyed our mutual enchantment with the French capital, including a shared fondness for a particular Left Bank bistro, where we each had dined. As a result I felt a warm kinship with her.

To be honest I've been guilty of the "Oh, that's nice" response – but no more! I'm asking many more questions now.

Finding answers to more questions. Pursuing answers to questions can have the same, wonderful impact on your life. How many times during the day have you stopped and asked, "Gee, I wonder why...or who...or what (fill in the blank)?" Researching the answers can lead to some very pleasant discoveries.

For instance, while hanging my flag one Fourth of July, I wondered: Do I display the flag with the stars on the right or the left? Enter the internet! Not only did I find the answer to my question, but I was also inspired to go deeper and – lo and behold – found myself immersed in flag history and etiquette.

The pleasant discovery? The experience not only expanded my knowledge; it also piqued my patriotism. My Fourth of July was richer for having answered my own question.

Changing things up. I'm also more determined now to do things I've never done before. Recently I read an article in the daily paper about the "reinvigoration" of a local Hindu temple. This ancient ritual is designed to restore the spiritual power of the temple and heal some of the world's ills.

Imagine my surprise (and delight) when I learned the temple was located just miles from my home. I decided to go. And what a good decision that was! I grabbed a friend, and together we entered a fascinating world of Hindu tradition and devotion, expressed in rhythmic chanting, bright colors, and the spicy aroma of fire-pit smoke.

We met gentle, beautiful people interested in helping us understand the powerful significance of this special event, and we left feeling more a part of the world.

Breaking some (little) rules. I'm not talking about anything that will land you behind bars; I'm talking about letting go of some self-imposed rules. Here's an example: For years, I had this "thing" about socializing with people from work. I made it off limits. I don't know exactly where that came from, but it kept me from forming some really nice relationships. I finally let go of that way of thinking and really enjoyed getting to know my colleagues better.

Think about your own life. Is a self-imposed rule keeping your life small? What would happen if you broke it? (Maybe you'll get a nice surprise!)

Being curious can lead to deeper relationships, as well as new ones. I've learned that curiosity can lead to places you've never been or a renewed appreciation for the paths you've already traveled. When you are open to new people, new experiences, and other points of view, you grow and learn about others, yourself, and the world at large. You become part of something bigger than yourself and, therefore, feel less alone and more connected.

This is what else I've learned: when a flag is displayed vertically, the stars should be in the upper left corner. Let freedom (and curiosity) ring!

WHAT YOU CAN DO TODAY

Ask yourself:

How would my life change (or get better) if I became a more curious person?

Now jot down one thing you will do today to cultivate your curious side.

_____

_____

_____

_____

_____

_____

_____

_____

_____

RENEW YOUR SPIRIT

For many women a new start is a perfect time to turn the page and vow to make some healthy changes.

My work with those who live alone has enriched my perspective on life and what it takes to be successful in the broadest sense of the word. Almost without exception the women who have found their way after a divorce or the death of a spouse have been bolstered by a healthy spiritual life.

Many of the participants in my workshops take good advantage of spiritual opportunities and occasions. They regularly attend worship services, find comfort in prayer and hymns, and faithfully observe religious holidays.

Others march to a different drummer and nourish their spiritual life in private moments: listening to music, communing with nature, reading or writing, or just sitting quietly in mindful meditation.

However expressed, my observations have shown me that those who nurture their spiritual lives fare better when challenged by life's transitions. I consider them fortunate – fortunate because they take time to renew their spirits and, by doing so, find inner strength to navigate uncharted waters and help others along the way.

Even when their own sense of self-worth is fragile or failing, I've seen devout divorcees and widows reach out to others with encouragement and prayer. Spiritually grounded, their empathy runs deep, and their desire to support others is steadfast.

Last month I heard from a woman whose husband abruptly left her and their three teenage children after 28 years of marriage. She was in shock and consumed with pain. She shared with me how comforting it would have been to hear from her minister and church friends, but they didn't know her situation. It had been years since she had been to church, and those relationships had fallen by the wayside.

Similarly, a neighbor of mine confided that he'd stopped going to temple after he lost his wife to breast cancer. Mad at the injustice of it all, he couldn't bring himself to attend services without her. This led to years of isolation, during which he was overcome with loneliness and guilt. I wasn't surprised when he talked of numbing his pain with alcohol.

My suggestion to both was simple: Renew your spiritual connections.

It's easy to imagine how difficult it might be to contact a minister, priest, rabbi, or other spiritual advisor and ask for help if you've been absent from services for many years – or when loneliness has you in its grip. But any religious organization worthy of its mission will respond with open arms. A warm embrace is waiting for the one who walks through the door.

Likewise, if other doors beckon – if nature or poetry or music feed your soul – go forth and embrace those opportunities. My spiritual battery gets recharged when I take time out from my busy schedule to be still and meditate. Quiet times in inspirational settings allow me to contemplate my most deeply held beliefs. I emerge grounded and motivated.

The power of a spiritual life is mighty. When you pursue your spiritual goals and teachings, life can become more manageable, and your ability to cope with loss, loneliness, and everyday struggles is strengthened.

Whatever form your pursuit takes, I encourage you to make that connection or reconnection now. Today. An idea bigger than yourself, a set of beliefs, and the company of people who share your faith can lead to a richer, more meaningful, and peaceful existence.

While you may live alone, you do not have to go through life alone. And what a blessing that is.

WHAT YOU CAN DO TODAY

Ask yourself:

Am I feeling empty and disconnected?

Now jot down one thing you will do today to nurture your spiritual life.

_____

_____

_____

_____

_____

_____

_____

_____

_____

SIX MONTHS FROM NOW...

It can be life changing to adopt a positive attitude anchored in gratitude.

I agree with author Norman Vincent Peale, who said, "Change your thoughts and you change your world." But I know, too, that it takes more than a sunny attitude to create the life you want. It also takes *action*.

In my workshops I lead groups through an empowering three-step exercise that helps women get "unstuck" and on the road to a happier, more fulfilled life.

The first step is to put it all out there. I ask participants to share their worst fears, their self-doubts, and the negative inner talk that gets in the way of feeling better and finding contentment. The replies usually sound like this:

I fear

- being lonely.
- that I've lost my confidence for good.
- no one caring about or missing me.
- dying alone, penniless, and miserable.

- eating alone forever.

- trudging through the holidays.

- being helpless when it comes to home repairs.

- never finding love again or feeling special, as if I'm "Number One."

- for my safety.

- feeling vulnerable.

- not having the know-how to manage my finances.

- losing all my energy and motivation.

- no one will be here to care for me if I get sick.

- a quiet house.

- never enjoying touch and affection again or being kissed good night.

- making big decisions by myself.

- becoming stagnant and not taking risks.

- never feeling joy again.

I'm always struck by the depth of the anguish. All these negative thoughts – while very real – are distressing. This is when I remind the group that healthy change and personal growth are next to impossible when immersed in negative thinking.

And so we switch direction.

My next question for the group: "How would you like to feel six months from now?" The response is heartening.

The women often tell me they want to feel

- calm, settled, at peace.

- more confident and courageous.

- more in touch with who they really are.

- able to accept their circumstances.

- more forgiving and trusting of others and themselves.

- proud of their behavior and seen by their children as role models.

- willing and able to help others.

- released from self-pity.

- competent, able to make decisions big and small.

- happier, able to enjoy things more easily.

- more in control and secure financially.

- adventuresome and open to life in general.

- healed and hopeful about the future.

- strong enough to reach out and invite people into their lives, perhaps even date.

- joyful, light, free.

Now that's more like it! The energy in the room changes for the good, and we're on a hopeful, more optimistic path.

I then ask the women to identify an action step (or steps) they can take to help them realize short-term goals. Some share their next steps with the group; others choose to keep their goals private. All are committed to taking at least one action step that will lead toward feeling better in the future.

This exercise really works. And you can do it on your own. I've been moved and inspired by the success stories I've heard from participants who have embraced living alone and taken deliberate strides toward improving their life circumstances and overall well-being.

Actions *do* speak louder than words. They also speak louder than loneliness, helplessness, and hopelessness. Take action today, and I'm confident you'll feel better – more whole and complete – in six months.

WHAT YOU CAN DO TODAY

Ask yourself:

How do I want to describe myself and my life six months from now?

Now jot down one thing you will do today to start making that vision a reality.

_____

_____

_____

_____

_____

_____

_____

_____

FINAL THOUGHTS AND WISHES

I hope the essays and exercises in this book have been a source of inspiration for you.

Each person's journey toward contentment is unique. Mine started with saying yes to life and pulling myself up and out of self-imposed isolation after my divorce. Yours may begin with a small step (changing a daily routine) or a big leap (moving to a new city). You know best.

Big or small, what matters is taking that first step during this life-changing chapter of your life. So start today. Rediscover yourself. And embrace your independence. I'm confident that joy and contentment will follow, wherever life and love take you.

ABOUT THE AUTHOR

Gwenn Voelckers is the founder and facilitator of Live Alone and Thrive empowerment workshops for women, a newspaper columnist, and a sought-after speaker. After her divorce she overcame loneliness and loss to create a life of fulfillment and joy on her own. Today she is dedicated to helping others embrace their independence and feel "at home" with themselves. Gwenn lives with her dog, Scout, in an 1830s English cottage in upstate New York, where she runs her workshops and operates House Content Bed & Breakfast.

Contact information
E-mail: gvoelckers@rochester.rr.com
Call: (585) 624-7887
Visit: www.aloneandcontent.com

Made in the USA
Middletown, DE
07 October 2020